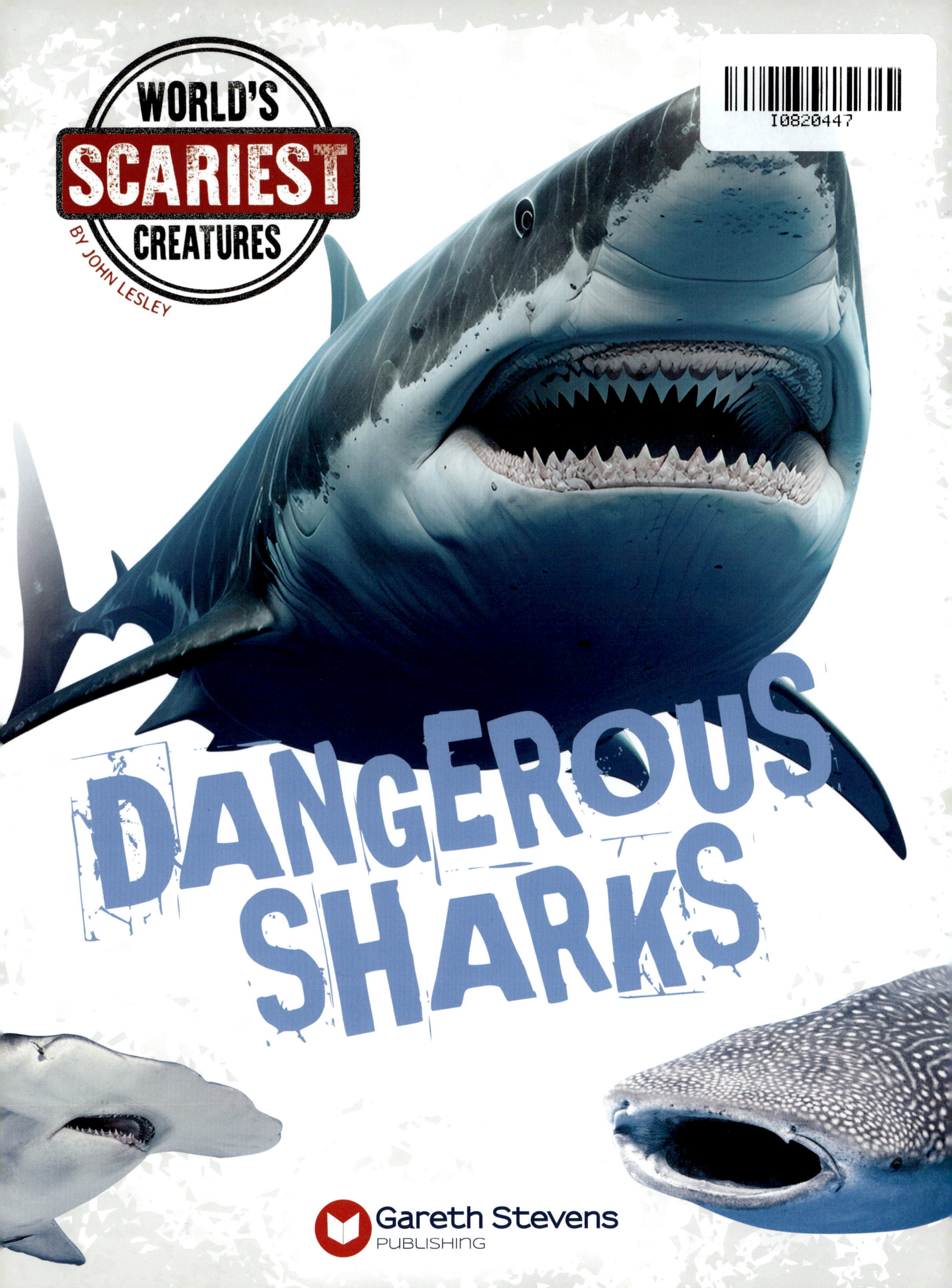

WORLD'S
SCARIEST
CREATURES
BY JOHN LESLEY
I0820447
DANGEROUS
SHARKS
Gareth Stevens
PUBLISHING

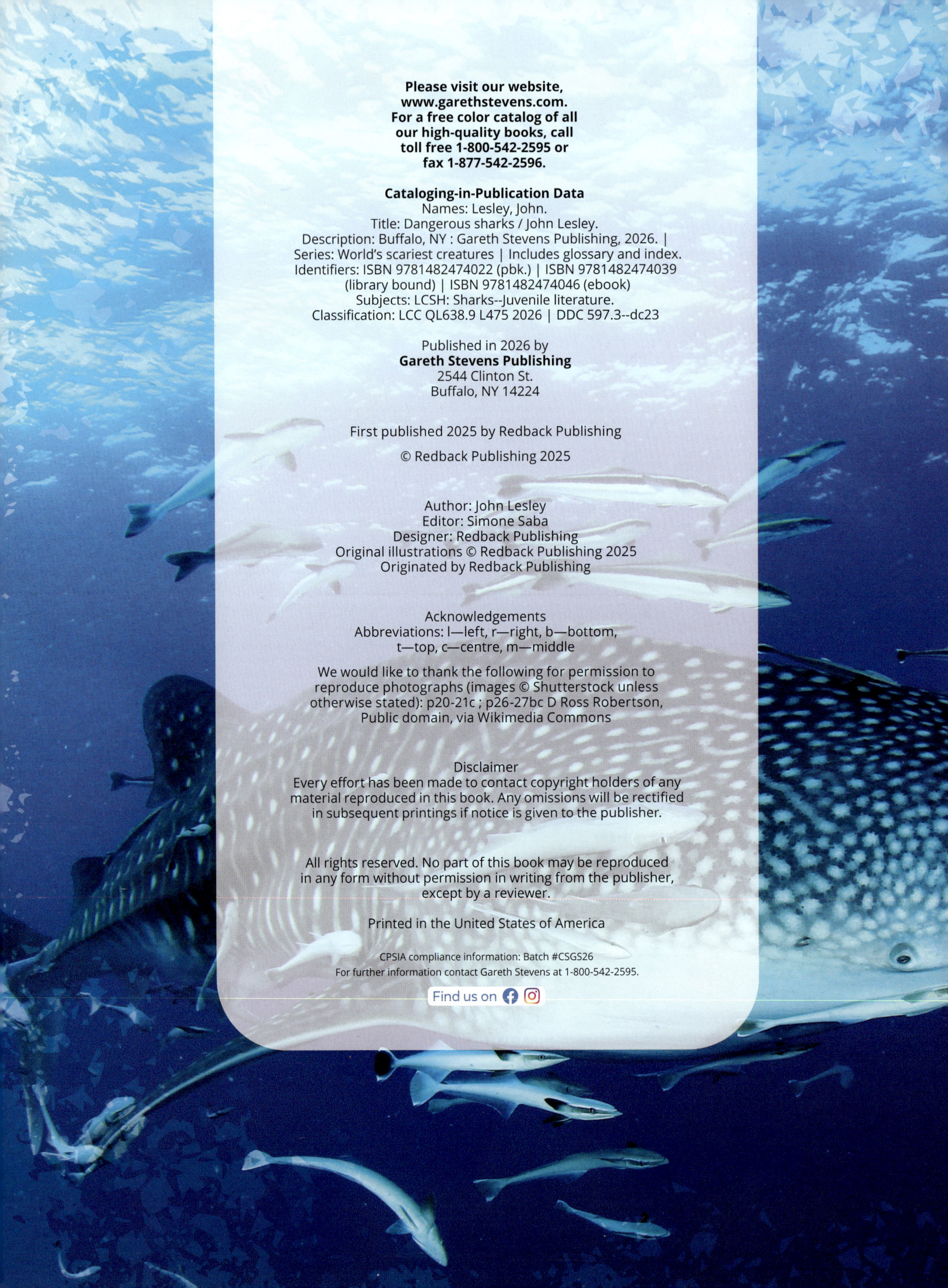

**Please visit our website,
www.garethstevens.com.
For a free color catalog of all
our high-quality books, call
toll free 1-800-542-2595 or
fax 1-877-542-2596.**

Cataloging-in-Publication Data
Names: Lesley, John.
Title: Dangerous sharks / John Lesley.
Description: Buffalo, NY : Gareth Stevens Publishing, 2026. | Series: World's scariest creatures | Includes glossary and index.
Identifiers: ISBN 9781482474022 (pbk.) | ISBN 9781482474039 (library bound) | ISBN 9781482474046 (ebook)
Subjects: LCSH: Sharks--Juvenile literature.
Classification: LCC QL638.9 L475 2026 | DDC 597.3--dc23

Published in 2026 by
Gareth Stevens Publishing
2544 Clinton St.
Buffalo, NY 14224

First published 2025 by Redback Publishing

Author: John Lesley
Editor: Simone Saba
Designer: Redback Publishing
Original illustrations © Redback Publishing 2025
Originated by Redback Publishing

Acknowledgements
Abbreviations: l—left, r—right, b—bottom, t—top, c—centre, m—middle

We would like to thank the following for permission to reproduce photographs (images © Shutterstock unless otherwise stated): p20-21c ; p26-27bc D Ross Robertson, Public domain, via Wikimedia Commons

Printed in the United States of America

CPSIA compliance information: Batch #CSGS26
For further information contact Gareth Stevens at 1-800-542-2595.

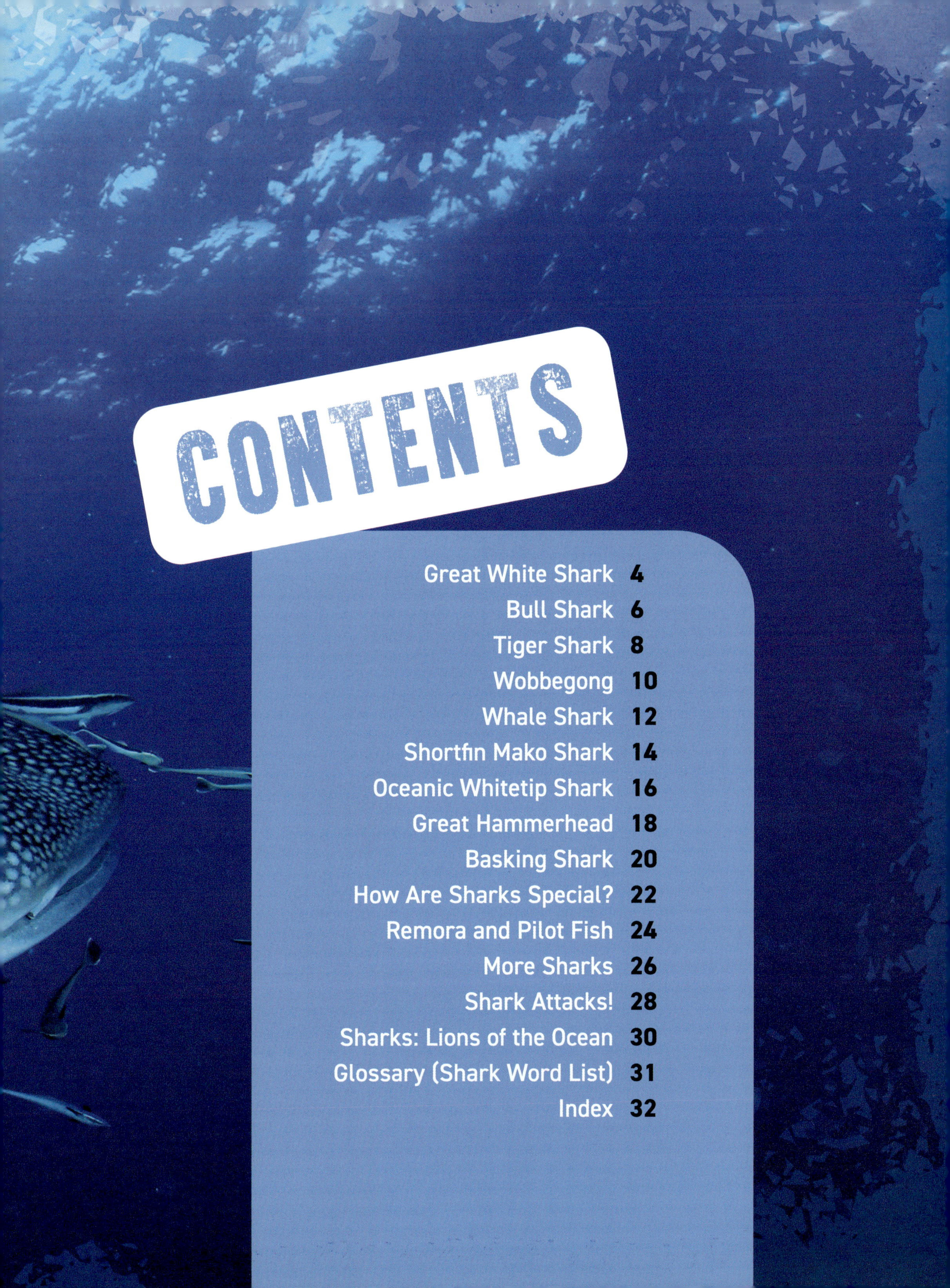

CONTENTS

Great White Shark 4
Bull Shark 6
Tiger Shark 8
Wobbegong 10
Whale Shark 12
Shortfin Mako Shark 14
Oceanic Whitetip Shark 16
Great Hammerhead 18
Basking Shark 20
How Are Sharks Special? 22
Remora and Pilot Fish 24
More Sharks 26
Shark Attacks! 28
Sharks: Lions of the Ocean 30
Glossary (Shark Word List) 31
Index 32

GREAT WHITE SHARK

Carcharodon carcharias

Great white sharks are one of the most fascinating and fearsome predators in the ocean. They can grow up to 20 feet (6 m) in length, and can weigh up to 5,000 pounds (2,268 kg).

BITING

Their teeth are large, serrated, and triangular, perfect for slicing through the flesh of their prey. They continuously lose and replace their teeth throughout their lives.

LIFE CYCLE

Great white sharks give birth to pups that are able to swim away and look after themselves immediately. They can live for over 50 years.

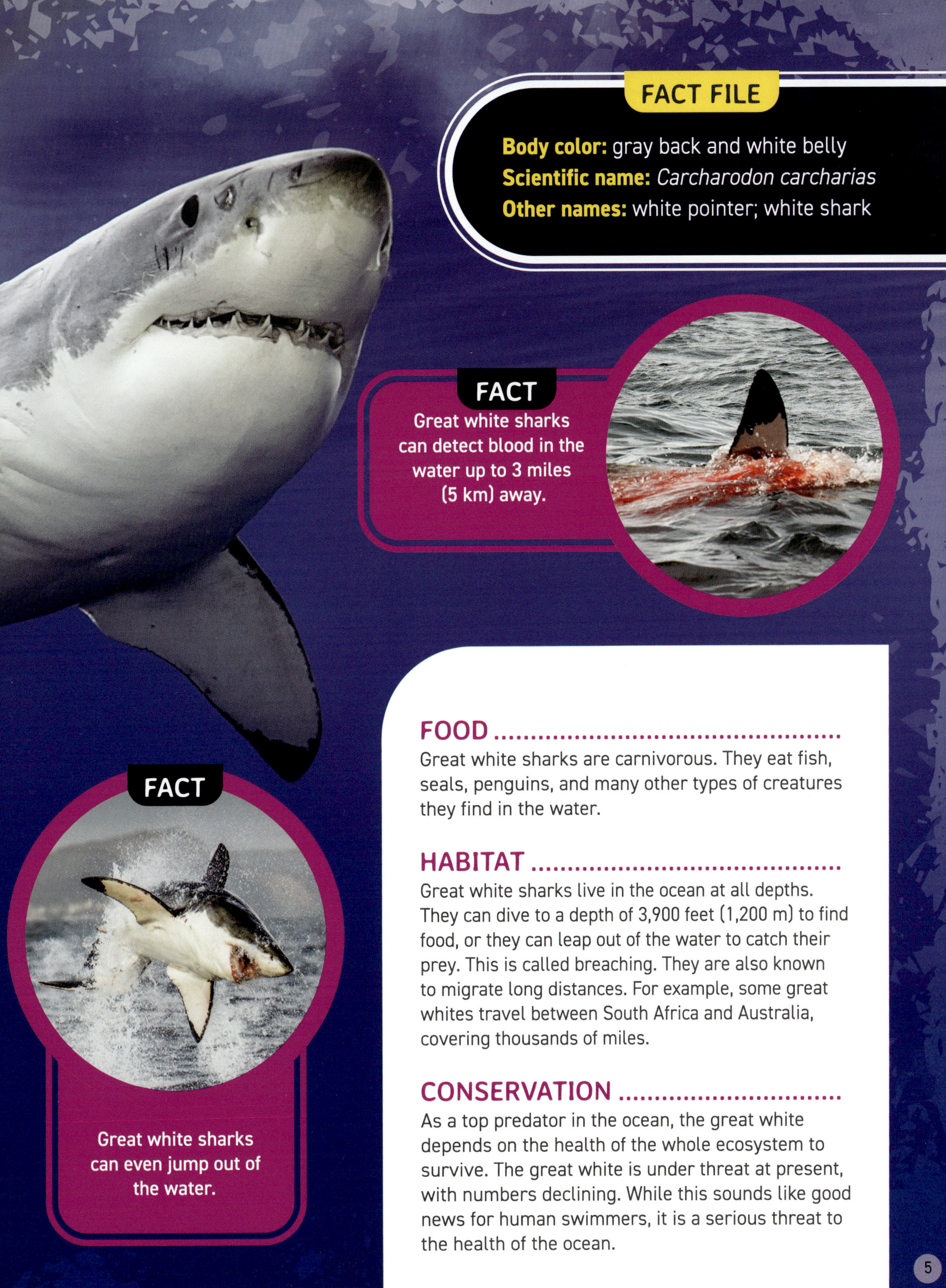

FACT FILE

Body color: gray back and white belly
Scientific name: *Carcharodon carcharias*
Other names: white pointer; white shark

FACT

Great white sharks can detect blood in the water up to 3 miles (5 km) away.

FACT

Great white sharks can even jump out of the water.

FOOD

Great white sharks are carnivorous. They eat fish, seals, penguins, and many other types of creatures they find in the water.

HABITAT

Great white sharks live in the ocean at all depths. They can dive to a depth of 3,900 feet (1,200 m) to find food, or they can leap out of the water to catch their prey. This is called breaching. They are also known to migrate long distances. For example, some great whites travel between South Africa and Australia, covering thousands of miles.

CONSERVATION

As a top predator in the ocean, the great white depends on the health of the whole ecosystem to survive. The great white is under threat at present, with numbers declining. While this sounds like good news for human swimmers, it is a serious threat to the health of the ocean.

BULL SHARK

Carcharhinus leucas

People often mistake bull sharks for great whites. Bull sharks can survive for long periods in fresh water, so if you spot a shark a long way from the ocean it is probably a bull shark.

Bull sharks have a sleek shape. They have a wide head, which is the main way to tell the difference between them and great whites.

LIFE CYCLE

Bull sharks can live for over 20 years. In the summer, they swim up rivers to give birth to their pups. A young bull shark is about 12 inches (30 cm) long. When it is small, the pup is safer in a river, rather than out in the open ocean, where there are many carnivores that would like to eat it. They eventually grow to about 9.8 feet (3 m) long.

FACT

Bull sharks are aggressive. They have attacked humans in rivers and harbors all around the world.

FACT FILE

Body color: gray back and lighter-colored belly
Scientific name: *Carcharhinus leucas*
Other names: river shark; swan river whaler; freshwater whaler

HABITAT

Bull sharks live in tropical and temperate oceans and rivers.

FOOD

Bull sharks are carnivores but probably do not hunt human swimmers as food. They tend to prefer smaller prey such as fish and crabs as meals. In rivers, they will eat any animal that goes into the water.

BITING

Bull sharks do bite and can cause very serious wounds.

TIGER SHARK

Galeocerdo cuvier

LIFE CYCLE

The female tiger shark produces live pups. Adults grow to about 16 feet (5 m) long and can weigh up to 1.1 tons (1 mt). They can live for well over 10 years.

HABITAT

Tiger sharks live in warm oceans and sometimes travel a short distance into rivers as well.

FOOD

Tiger sharks hunt and eat everything from crabs to fish, turtles, dolphins, seals, and seabirds. They will also feed on dead animals in the water. Their well-developed senses allow them to hunt in the dark by sensing tiny movements in the water, as well as the electric fields created by other animals nearby. They have an acute sense of smell, particularly for blood in the water.

BITING

Tiger sharks are very dangerous and will attack a human swimmer. They will test large prey by bumping their snout against it before biting.

FACT

The tiger shark's teeth are sharp and point sideways, which gives them greater power to rip through flesh.

FACT FILE

Body color: blue-gray with darker gray stripes
Scientific name: *Galeocerdo cuvier*
Other names: commonly called the "man-eater" shark

The tiger shark is such a ferocious eater that it often swallows ocean garbage.

FACT

The tiger shark is one of the three most dangerous in the world for human swimmers.

WOBBEGONG

Orectolobus

Wobbegongs are classified in the genus *Orectolobus*. They are sometimes called carpet sharks because of the patterns on their skin.

Wobbegongs do not roam the ocean like great whites. They prefer to wait for food to come near them, and then they pounce on it. Their mottled coloring helps them to blend in with their surroundings. Sometimes they even let sand cover and hide them. Then they grab any fish or crab that comes close. They have many skin flaps around their mouth, which may send them information about their surroundings. Their rounded fins are like paddles and are also useful for pushing the shark across the sea floor when hunting.

LIFE CYCLE

Wobbegongs can grow to 9.8 feet (3 m) long and weigh as much as a human adult. They produce live young.

HABITAT

The wobbegong, or carpet shark, lives on the sea floor in warm and temperate regions.

FACT

The name wobbegong may be an Australian Aboriginal word meaning "beard," in reference to the little flaps of skin around the shark's mouth.

FACT

Once a wobbegong bites, it will not let go, so stay away if you see one.

FOOD

Wobbegongs are carnivores. They eat mainly fish and crabs.

CONSERVATION

Wobbegongs used to be under threat of extinction, but their numbers have increased, and populations seem to be safe for the moment.

BITING

Wobbegongs have sharp teeth. They will bite a human if annoyed or threatened by them. Their wide, flat head covers a huge mouth, full of sharp teeth.

WHALE SHARK

Rhincodon typus

FACT

The whale shark is the biggest fish in the ocean.

The whale shark is the biggest fish in the ocean, and it can grow to over 46 feet (14 m) long. It is not a whale, but a fish with cartilage instead of hard bones in its body.

LIFE CYCLE

Whale sharks can live for over 80 years. Females give birth to multiple, live pups, each up to 3.3 feet (1 m) long.

FOOD

The whale shark is a filter feeder. It strains small creatures out of the water and does not hunt and kill prey the way that other sharks do. The head is very wide and heavy, as it has to house the extremely large mouth and the food-filtering structures. Whale sharks can suck in huge volumes of water, but they don't like any big animal getting into their mouth.

Since they do not have any teeth and do not hunt for food, whale sharks do not attack and bite people. However, the whale shark is so enormous, that divers swimming too close have been injured by the body or fin of a whale shark.

FACT

Whale sharks dive straight down to a depth of 6,560 feet (2 km)!

FACT FILE

Body color: dark gray with lighter-colored spots
Scientific name: *Rhincodon typus*

FACT

Human divers who get too close risk being sucked towards a whale shark's mouth by accident!

HABITAT

Whale sharks live in warm, tropical oceans.

CONSERVATION

Whale sharks are endangered. The reasons for this include:

- Pollution of the oceans
- Threats to their food sources from ocean warming
- Increased commercial fishing that takes the same food that whale sharks eat

SHORTFIN MAKO SHARK

Isurus oxyrinchus

Shortfin mako sharks are among the fastest sharks, capable of swimming at speeds of up to 45 miles (72 km) per hour. This speed helps them catch fast-moving prey such as tuna and swordfish.

LIFE CYCLE

The female shark gives birth to live pups that are fully developed and independent. Shortfin mako sharks can live up to 30 years or more in the wild.

HABITAT

Shortfin mako sharks are found in temperate and tropical waters worldwide. They inhabit offshore open waters but can sometimes be seen near the coast.

FOOD

Their diet includes fish (tuna, mackerel, and swordfish), squid, and other cephalopods. They have also been known to consume smaller sharks and marine mammals.

FACT

Shortfin mako sharks are capable of leaping up to 20 feet (6 m) out of the water.

FACT FILE

Body color: metallic blue coloration on their back and sides, with a white underbelly
Scientific name: *Isurus oxyrinchus*
Size: up to 13 feet (4 m) long and weighing around 1,300 pounds (590 kg)

FACT

Shortfin mako sharks have long, slender, and very sharp teeth that protrude from their mouths even when closed.

OCEANIC WHITETIP SHARK

Carcharhinus longimanus

Oceanic whitetip sharks are known for their aggressive behavior, particularly in situations where food is present, such as around shipwrecks. These sharks are apex predators that love the wide-open ocean. The tips of their dorsal, pectoral, pelvic, and caudal fins are often marked with white spots, giving them their name.

LIFE CYCLE

The young are born live, fully developed, and independent. They can grow up to 13 feet (4 m) long and weigh around 370 pounds (167 kg).

HABITAT

Oceanic whitetip sharks are found in tropical and subtropical waters worldwide, particularly in the open ocean.

FACT

They are known to be aggressive towards humans.

FACT FILE

Body color: bronze or grayish-blue dorsal side and a white underbelly

Scientific name: *Carcharhinus longimanus*

Size: up to 13 feet (4 m) long and weighing around 370 pounds (167 kg)

FACT

They are often accompanied by pilot fish, which feed on parasites and leftovers from the shark's meals.

GREAT HAMMERHEAD

Sphyrna mokarran

FACT

Hammerheads can see almost completely around themselves.

FACT

The hammerhead brain is the most developed of any shark. This means it is both smart and dangerous.

The defining feature of a hammerhead shark is that its eyes are at the ends of extensions that stick out from each side of the head. This adaptation improves its ability to see what is around it.

The strange, unwieldy appearance of the hammerhead shark does not make it any less fierce than its more streamlined shark relatives. The hammerhead is just as fast and dangerous.

FACT FILE

Body color: plain gray back and lighter-colored belly

Scientific name: *Sphyrna mokarran*

FOOD

Hammerheads hunt for fish, crabs, and squid.

LIFE CYCLE

Female hammerheads give birth to numerous pups. So that the pups' eyes are not damaged, the extensions are bent backwards for protection during birth. Adults grow to about 20 feet (6 m) long.

HABITAT

Hammerheads like to be in warm waters, both near the coast and in the open ocean. They often congregate in large groups of over a hundred sharks.

BITING

Hammerheads might bite humans if they find them in the water near a shoal of fish, or if there is blood in the water.

FACT

Hammerheads can sense Earth's magnetic field, and probably use this as a road map during their long migrations through the oceans.

BASKING SHARK

Cetorhinus maximus

GENTLE GIANTS

Despite their size, basking sharks are not dangerous to humans and have a gentle nature.

The basking shark is the second-largest living shark and fish species. It is known for its enormous size and gentle nature. Basking sharks can grow up to 40 feet (12 m) in length and can weigh up to 11,000 pounds (5,000 kg)!

LIFE CYCLE

Female basking sharks produce eggs that hatch inside their body. When they are big enough to live independently in the ocean, they are born. This is called ovoviviparous reproduction.

LONG MIGRATIONS

Basking sharks are known for their long migrations, sometimes traveling thousands of miles to follow plankton blooms.

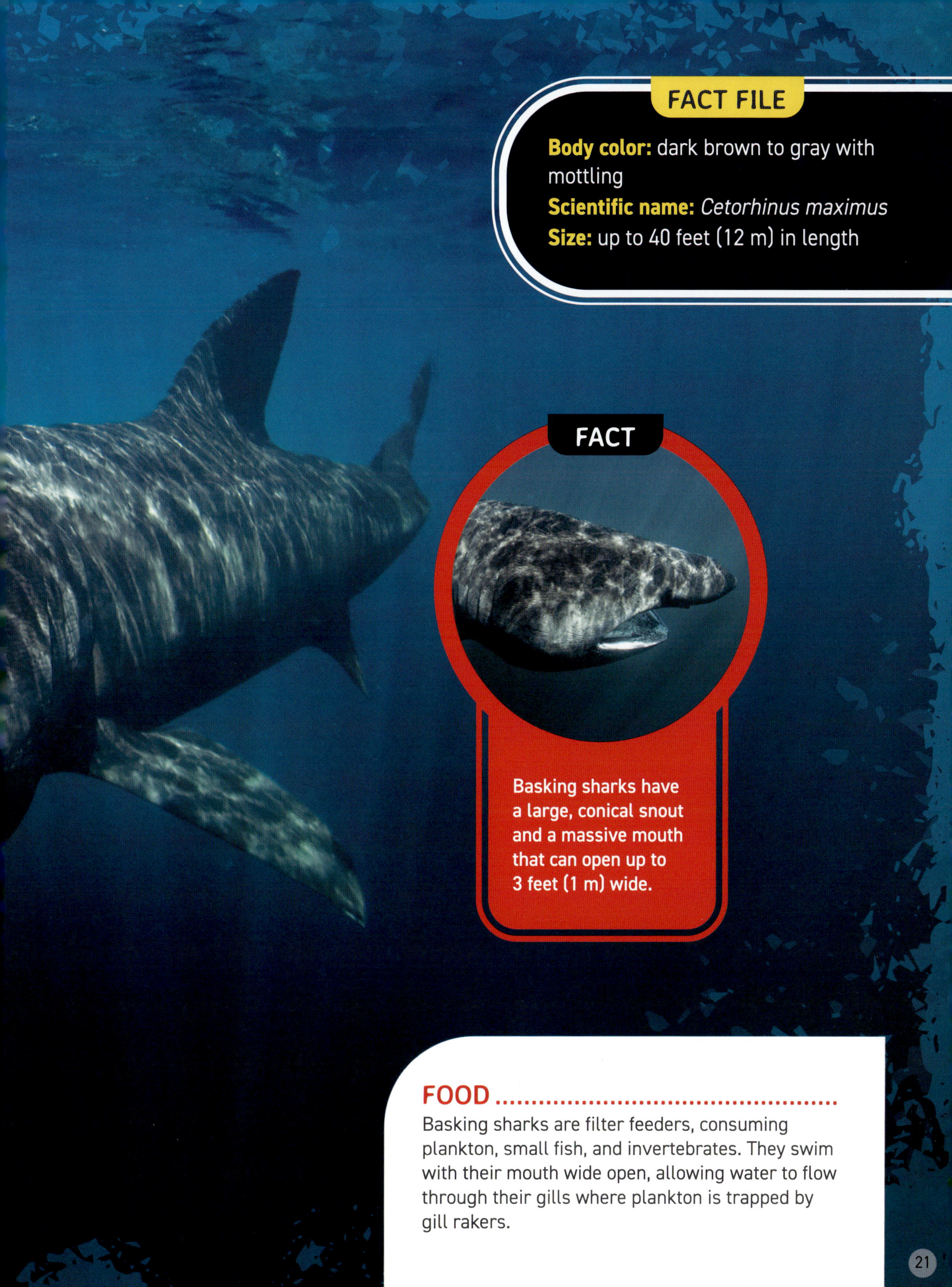

FACT FILE

Body color: dark brown to gray with mottling

Scientific name: *Cetorhinus maximus*

Size: up to 40 feet (12 m) in length

FACT

Basking sharks have a large, conical snout and a massive mouth that can open up to 3 feet (1 m) wide.

FOOD

Basking sharks are filter feeders, consuming plankton, small fish, and invertebrates. They swim with their mouth wide open, allowing water to flow through their gills where plankton is trapped by gill rakers.

HOW ARE SHARKS SPECIAL?

ON THE MOVE

Sharks do not have lungs. They need to keep moving to get oxygen out of the water as it passes over their gills. While small sharks can stay still for a while, larger sharks, such as the great white, must move constantly or they will drown.

Sharks have cartilage instead of bone. Cartilage is a strong, flexible connective tissue that absorbs impact better than bone. Humans have cartilage in the flexible parts of their ear and nose structures.

Sharks do not have scales like fish, but their skin has many tiny, sharp bumps instead.

MERMAID'S PURSE

REPRODUCTION

Sharks reproduce in two ways. Some give birth to live pups that swim away as soon as they are born. Other sharks produce a leathery pouch, sometimes called a mermaid's purse, that protects the developing embryo until the baby shark hatches. These purses are sometimes found washed up on beaches.

ANCIENT

Sharks are a very ancient type of animal. They were around long before the dinosaurs, and even before there were any trees or flowers on Earth.

Sharks can feel electromagnetism from other animals around them in the ocean.

Most sharks have many rows of sharp, triangular teeth. As the older, worn teeth fall out, they are replaced by a new row.

Sharks are fish, not mammals like whales.

SHARK FINNING

This practice involves cutting off sharks' fins, then dumping the shark back into the sea to die. It is illegal in some places. The fins are used for soup or for traditional medicine in some parts of the world.

REMORA AND PILOT FISH

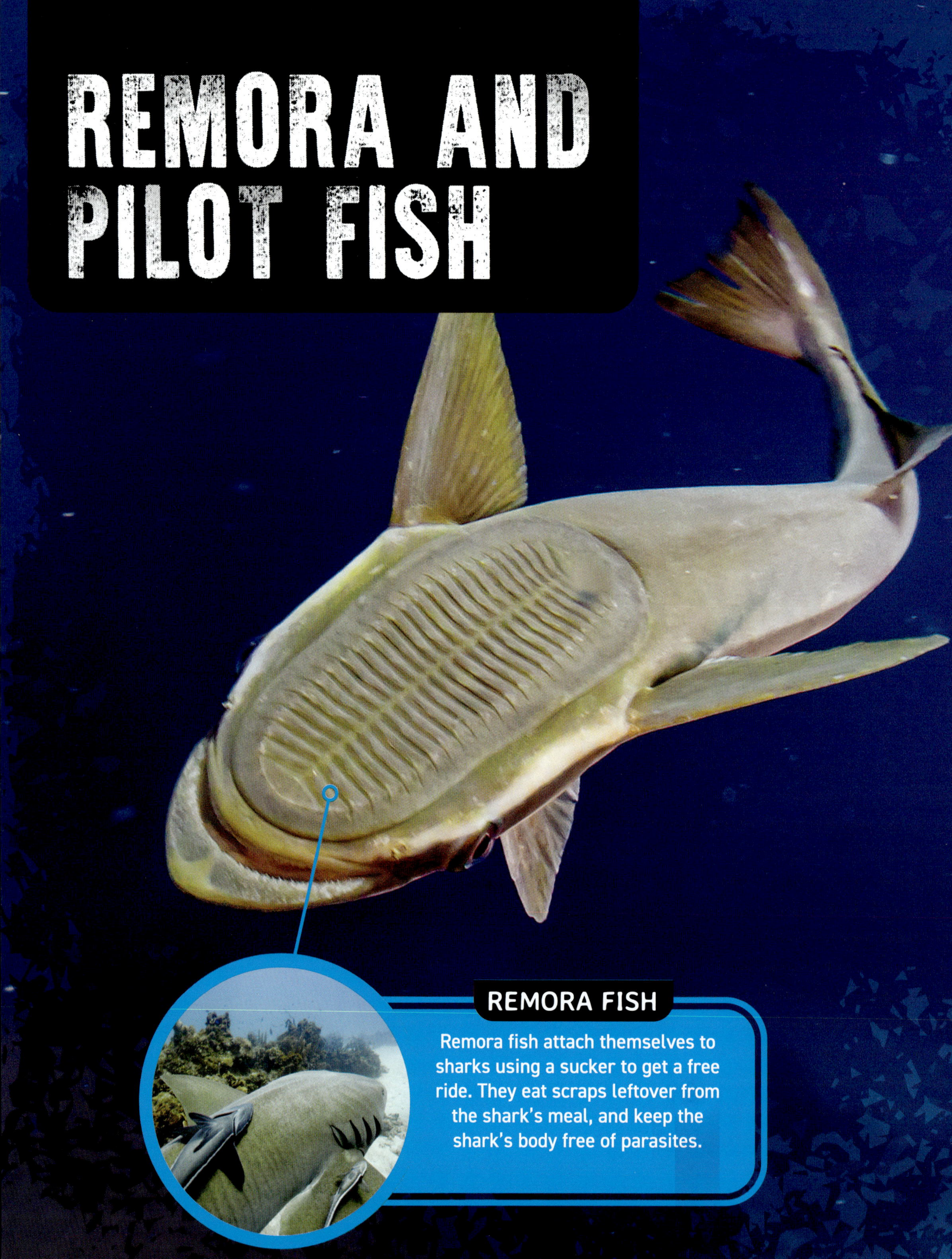

REMORA FISH

Remora fish attach themselves to sharks using a sucker to get a free ride. They eat scraps leftover from the shark's meal, and keep the shark's body free of parasites.

PILOT FISH

Pilot fish often tag along with sharks. They swim out of reach of the shark's jaws but follow them to pick up leftover food and gain protection from predators. A shark that is not hungry may allow a pilot fish to swim into its mouth to eat any parasites living in there.

MORE SHARKS

BLACKTIP SHARK
BRONZE WHALER SHARK
BLIND SHARK
SCHOOL SHARK

SHARK ATTACKS!

Great white sharks have been responsible for the highest number of shark bites of a person each year. Bull sharks and tiger sharks come in second and third.

The United States had the highest number of shark attack reports in the world in 2024 at 28. There were 36 reported in the United States in 2023. Many shark bites occur in the waters around the state of Florida.

The country with the next highest number of reported shark attacks is Australia. However, the risk of being attacked by a shark is very low.

AVOID A SHARK ATTACK

- Swim at patrolled beaches
- Swim with another person
- Don't swim when there are lots of fish in the water
- Don't swim at night, dawn, or dusk
- Don't swim in water where fishers have been cleaning their catch

SHARKS: LIONS OF THE OCEAN

Large sharks are often called the lions of the ocean. This is because lions and sharks are both top predators in their environments. Being at the top of their food chains, they play important roles in keeping the animals they prey on strong and healthy.

How can that be? They eat them, but they keep them healthy? YES!

By preying on the weaker and slower animals in a species, both lions and sharks serve the purpose that is common to all top predators. They feed on the slower and weaker animals, which results in the fitter and faster being the ones that escape to produce more offspring. Over time, this makes the whole population of prey animals stronger.

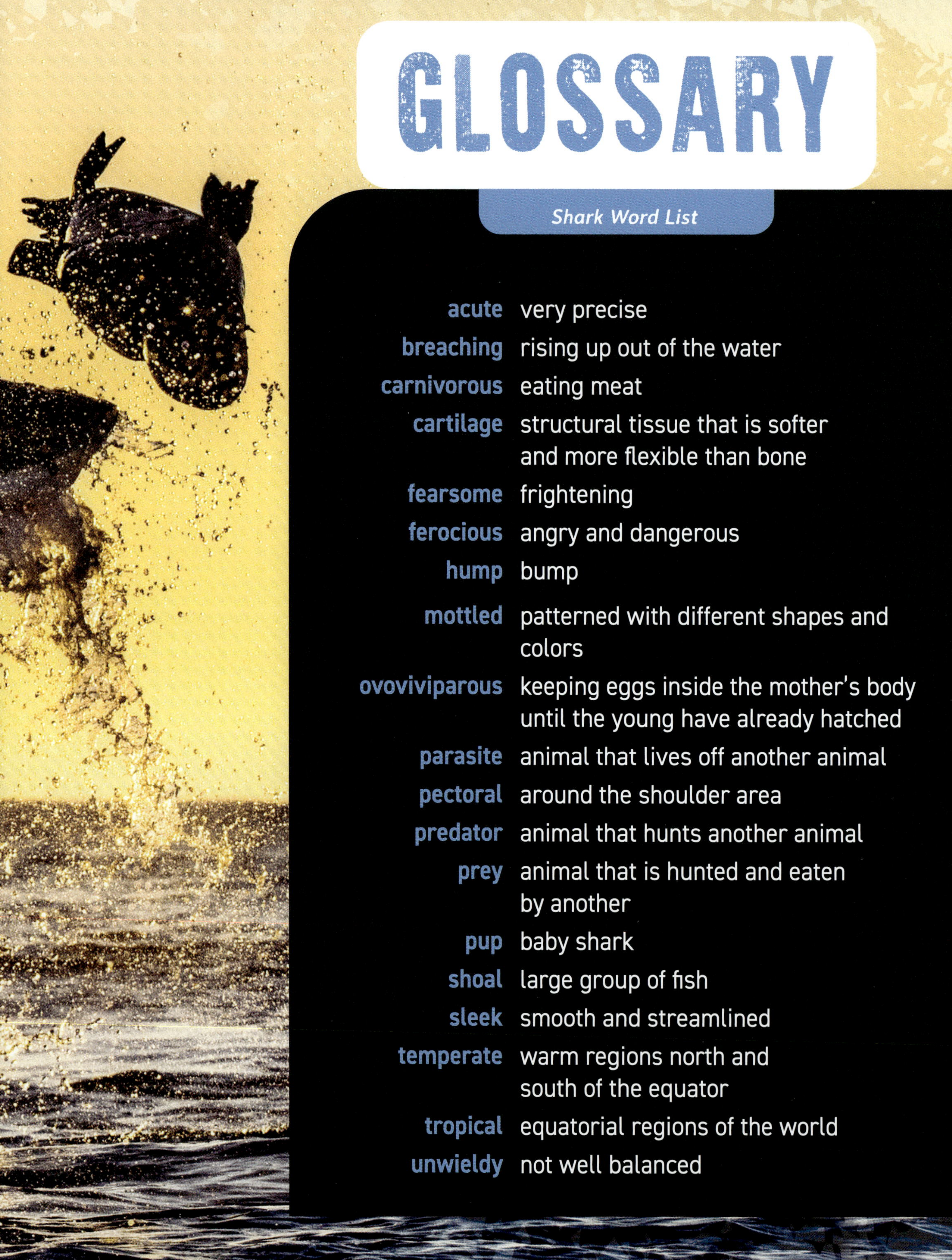

GLOSSARY

Shark Word List

acute very precise

breaching rising up out of the water

carnivorous eating meat

cartilage structural tissue that is softer and more flexible than bone

fearsome frightening

ferocious angry and dangerous

hump bump

mottled patterned with different shapes and colors

ovoviviparous keeping eggs inside the mother's body until the young have already hatched

parasite animal that lives off another animal

pectoral around the shoulder area

predator animal that hunts another animal

prey animal that is hunted and eaten by another

pup baby shark

shoal large group of fish

sleek smooth and streamlined

temperate warm regions north and south of the equator

tropical equatorial regions of the world

unwieldy not well balanced

INDEX

aggressive 6, 16, 17
carpet shark 10, 11, 12
cartilage 12, 22, 31
eggs 20, 31
electromagnetism 23
fins 10, 16, 23
jaws 25
mermaid's purse 22
people 6, 12, 28
prey 4, 5, 7, 8, 12, 14, 30, 31
pup 4, 6, 8, 12, 14, 19, 22, 31
rivers 6-8, 28
teeth 4, 8, 11, 12, 15, 23